PIANO SOLO

THE WORLD'S FAVORITE
CLASSICAL THEMES

ISBN 0-634-01696-2

HAL•LEONARD®
CORPORATION
7777 W. BLUEMOUND RD. P.O. BOX 13819 MILWAUKEE, WI 53213

Visit Hal Leonard Online at
www.halleonard.com

THE WORLD'S FAVORITE
CLASSICAL THEMES

CONTENTS

Air on the G String

from the Orchestral Suite No. 3 in D

Johann Sebastian Bach
1685-1750
BWV 1068
originally for orchestra

Jesu, Joy of Man's Desiring

Jesus bleibet meine Freude

from Cantata No. 147, HERZ UND MUND UND TAT UND LEBEN

Johann Sebastian Bach
1685-1750
BWV 147
originally for choir and orchestra

Prelude in C Major
from THE WELL-TEMPERED CLAVIER, BOOK 1

Johann Sebastian Bach
1685-1750

Adagio cantabile

Second Movement from Piano Sonata in C Minor, Op.13

Ludwig van Beethoven
1770-1827

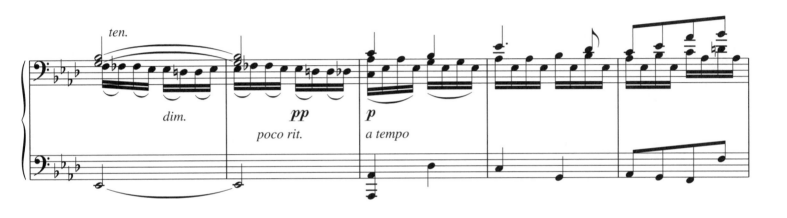

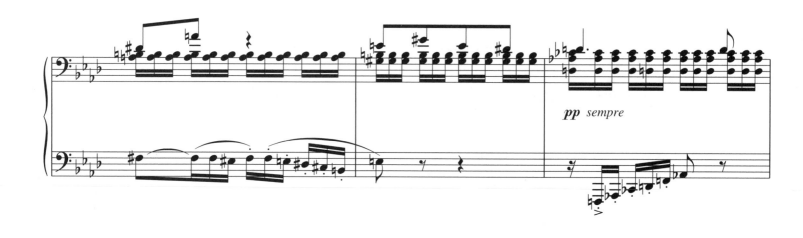

Für Elise
(For Elise)

Ludwig van Beethoven
1770-1827
WoO 59

Symphony No. 5 in C Minor

First Movement Excerpt

Ludwig van Beethoven
1770-1827
Op. 67
originally for orchestra

Habanera
from the opera *Carmen*

Georges Bizet
1838-1875

Polovetzian Dances

from the opera *Prince Igor*

First Theme

Alexander Borodin
1833-1887
originally for orchestra

Lullaby
(Wiegenlied)

Johannes Brahms
1830-1897
Op. 49, No. 4
originally for voice and piano

Waltz in A-flat Major

Johannes Brahms
1833-1897
Op. 39, No. 15

Prelude in A Major

Fryderyk Chopin
1810-1849
Op. 28, No. 7

Prelude in C Minor

Fryderyk Chopin
1810-1849
Op. 28, No. 20

Prelude in E Minor

Fryderyk Chopin
1810-1849
Op. 28, No. 4

Largo

The Girl with the Flaxen Hair

(La fille aux cheveux de lin)

Claude Debussy
1862-1918

Très calme et doucement expressif (♩ = 66)

Cédez   au Mouv !

très doux

Murmuré et en retenant peu à peu

Rêverie

Claude Debussy
1862-1918

Andante sans lenteur (not too slowly)

pp *très doux et très expressif*
(gently, expressively)

meno p

mf

dim.

Pizzicato Polka
from the ballet *Sylvia*

Léo Delibes
1836-1891

Allegretto ben moderato

Symphony No. 9 in E Minor

"From the New World"
Second Movement Excerpt ("Largo")

Antonín Dvořák
1841-1904
Op. 95
originally for orchestra

50

Funeral March of a Marionette

Themes

Charles Gounod
1818-1893
originally for orchestra

In the Hall of the Mountain King

from *Peer Gynt*

Edvard Grieg
1843-1907
Op. 23, No. 7
originally for orchestra

Alla marcia e molto marcato

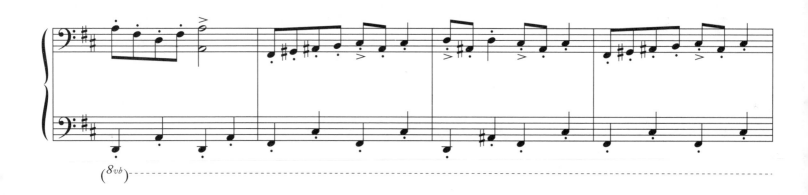

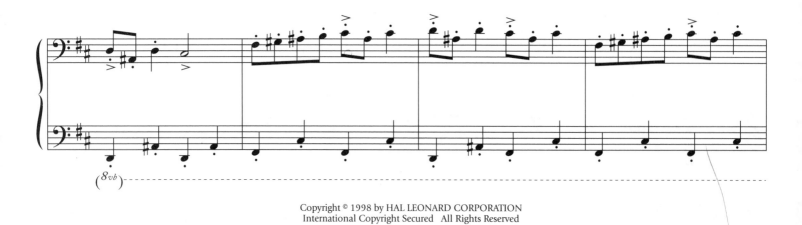

poco a poco cresc. e stretto

mf e sempre cresc.

Solvejg's Song

from *Peer Gynt*

Edvard Grieg
1843-1907
Op. 23, No. 20
originally for soprano and orchestra

Symphony No. 94 in G Major

"Surprise"
Second Movement Excerpt

Franz Joseph Haydn
1732-1809
originally for orchestra

Andante

Symphony No. 104 in D Major

"London"

First Movement Excerpt

Franz Joseph Haydn
1732-1809
originally for orchestra

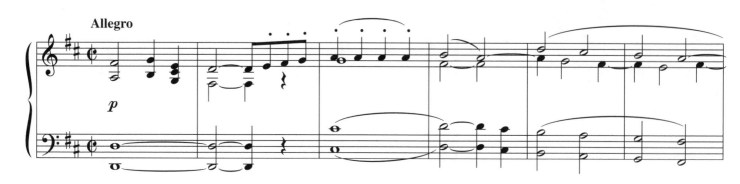

Evening Prayer
from the opera *Hänsel und Gretel*

Engelbert Humperdinck
1854-1921

Allegro maestoso
from WATER MUSIC
Excerpt

George Frideric Handel
1685-1759
originally for orchestra

Largo

"Ombra mai fù" from the opera *Serse*

George Frideric Handel
1685–1759

Larghetto

Hallelujah

from *Messiah*

George Frideric Handel
1685-1759
originally for chorus and orchestra

Allegro moderato

The Merry Widow
Selected Melodies

Franz Lehár
1870–1948

Allegretto moderato

"Silly Cavalier"

Tempo di Valse Lente
"For I Love You So"

a tempo

ritard.

rall.

Tempo di Valse lente
"The Merry Widow Waltz"

rit.

pp

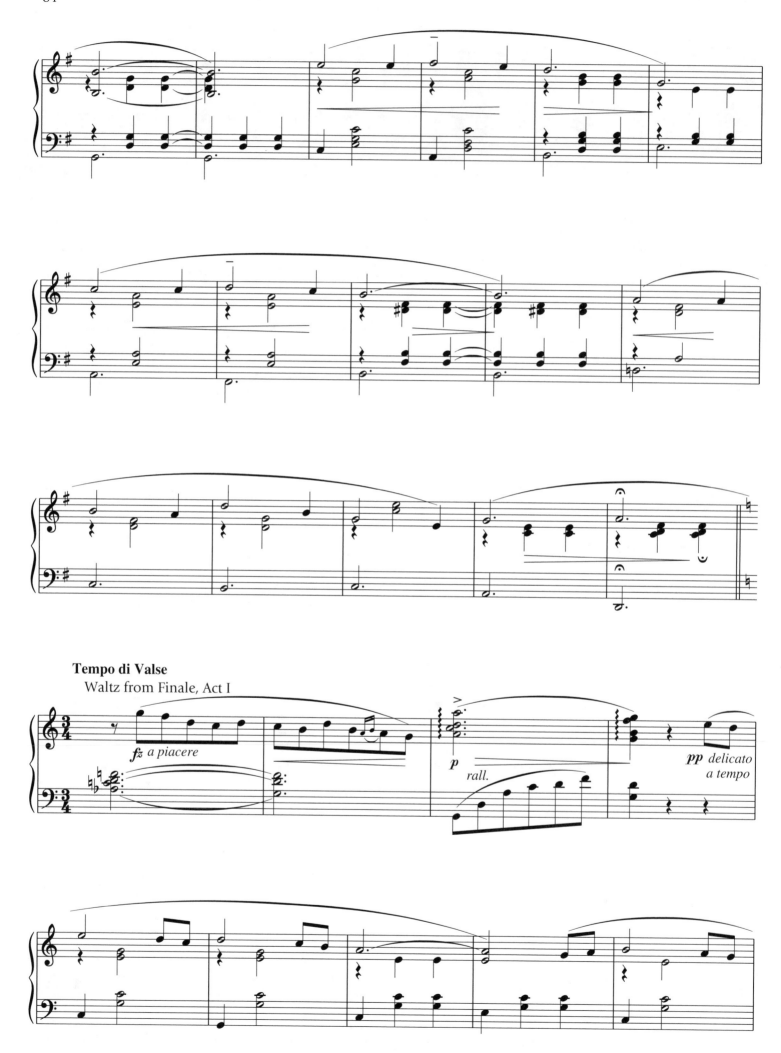

Tempo di Valse

Waltz from Finale, Act I

Andantino
"Vilia"

Allegro

"The Study of Woman"

Wedding March

from *A Midsummer Night's Dream*

Felix Mendelssohn
1809–1847

D.S. al Fine

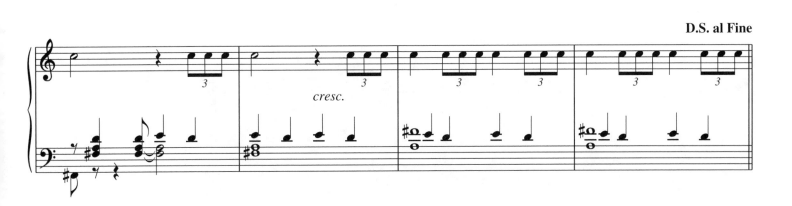

Rondeau

Excerpt

Jean-Joseph Mouret
1682–1738

Meditation
from the opera *Thaïs*

Jules Massenet
1842–1912

Eine kleine Nachtmusik

(A Little Night Music)
First Movement Excerpt

Wolfgang Amadeus Mozart
1756-1791
K 525
originally for string ensemble

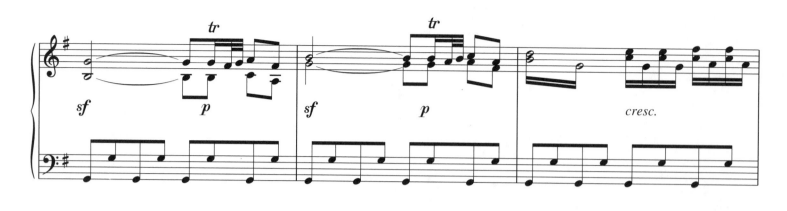

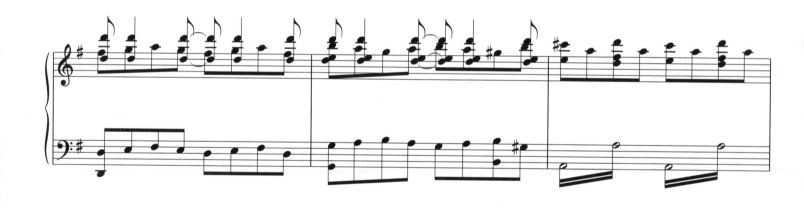

Alleluia

from the solo motet EXSULTATE, JUBILATE
Excerpt

Wolfgang Amadeus Mozart
1756-1791
K 165
originally for soprano and orchestra

Piano Concerto No. 21 in C Major

"Elvira Madigan"
Second Movement Excerpt

Wolfgang Amadeus Mozart
1756-1791
K 467
originally for piano and orchestra

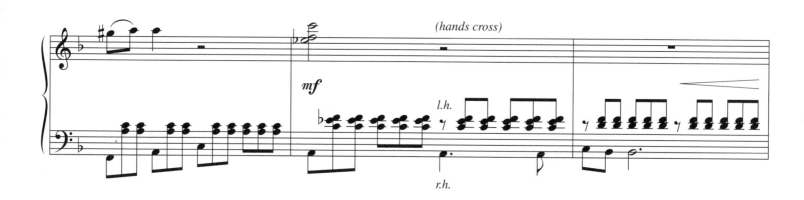

Sonata in C Major
First Movement

Wolfgang Amadeus Mozart
1756–1791
K 545

Barcarolle

from the opera *Les Contes D'Hoffmann*
(The Tales of Hoffmann)

Jacques Offenbach
1819–1880

Canon in D Major

Johann Pachelbel
1653-1706
originally for 3 violins and continuo

123

O mio babbino caro

from the opera *Gianni Schicchi*

Giacomo Puccini
1858-1924

Quando men vo

"Musetta's Waltz"
from the opera *La Bohème*

Giacomo Puccini
1858-1924

Trumpet Tune

Henry Purcell
1659–1695

Ave Maria

Franz Schubert
1797-1828
D. 839
originally for voice and piano

Serenade
(Ständchen)

Franz Schubert
1797-1828
D. 957, No. 4
originally for voice and piano

The Swan
from CARNIVAL OF THE ANIMALS

Camille Saint-Saëns
1835-1921
originally for chamber ensemble

By the Beautiful Blue Danube

Themes

Johann Strauss, Jr.
1825-1899
Op. 317
originally for orchestra

Tales from the Vienna Woods

Themes

Johann Strauss, Jr.
1825-1899
Op. 325
originally for orchestra

HMS Pinafore

Selected Melodies

Arthur Sullivan
1842–1900

Allegro
"We Sail the Ocean Blue"

Andante
"Sorry Her Lot"

149

152

Allegretto
"I am the Captain of the Pinafore"

Maestoso
"For He is an Englishman"

Dance of the Reed-Flutes

from the ballet *The Nutcracker*

Pyotr Il'yich Tchaikovsky
1840–1893

154

157

Dance of the Sugar Plum Fairy

from the ballet *The Nutcracker*

Pyotr Il'yich Tchaikovsky
1840–1893

Andante ma non troppo

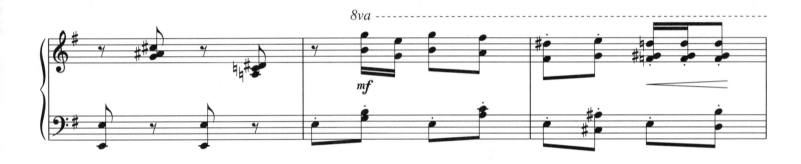

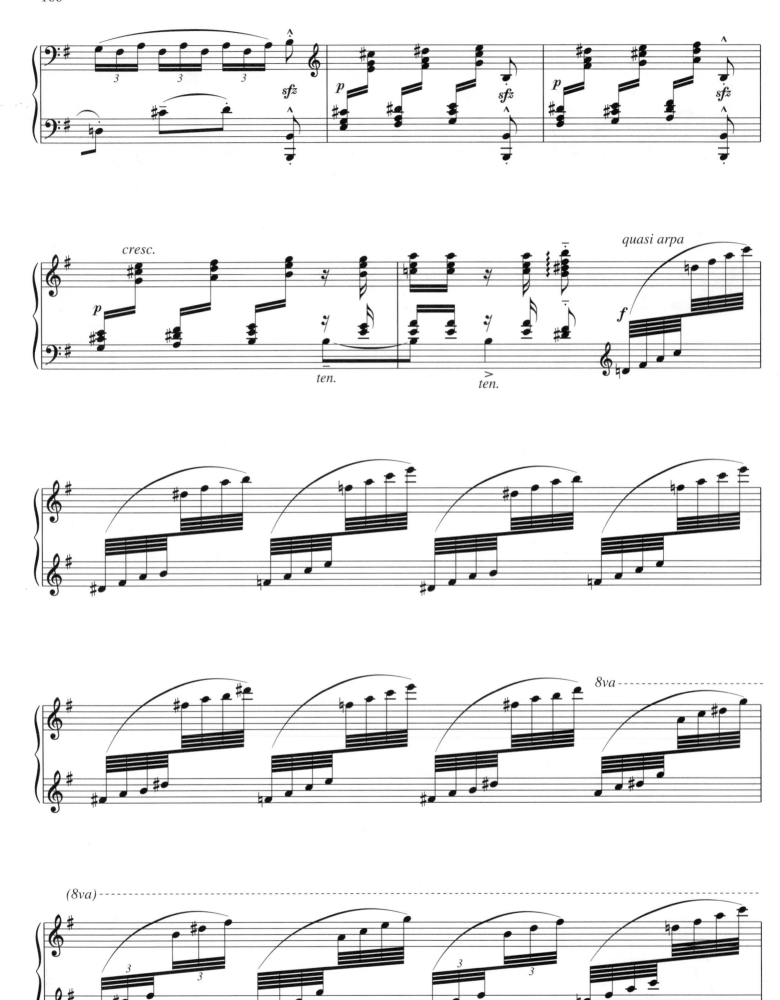

The Sleeping Beauty Waltz

from the ballet *The Sleeping Beauty*

Pyotr Il'yich Tchaikovsky
1840-1893
Op. 66
originally for orchestra

Bridal Chorus

from the opera *Lohengrin*

Richard Wagner
1813–1883

Addio, del passatto

from the opera *La Traviata* (The Fallen Woman)

Giuseppe Verdi
1813-1901

La donna è mobile

from the opera *Rigoletto*

Giuseppe Verdi
1813-1901

The Four Seasons

"Autumn"
First Movement Excerpt

Antonio Vivaldi
1678-1741
Op. 8, No. 3
originally for violin and orchestra